The Three Little Pigs

FULL-COLOR STURDY BOOK

Valeri Gorbachev

DOVER PUBLICATIONS, INC.
New York

Once upon a time there was an old sow with three little pigs. Since she was very poor and could not support them, she sent them off to seek their fortunes. The first little pig met a man with a bundle of straw, and said to him:

"Please, sir, let me have that straw so I can build myself a house."

Which the man did, and the little pig built himself a house with it.

*P*resently a wolf came along, and knocked at the door, and said:

"Little pig, little pig, let me come in."

To which the pig answered:

"No, no, not by the hair of my chinny chin chin."

The wolf then answered:

"Then I'll huff, and I'll puff, and I'll blow your house in."

So he huffed, and he puffed, and he blew the house in, and ate up the little pig.

The second little pig met a man with a bundle of sticks, and said:

"Please, sir, give me those sticks so I can build myself a house."

Which the man did, and the pig built his house. Then along came the wolf, and said:

"Little pig, little pig, let me come in."

"No, no, not by the hair of my chinny chin chin."

"Then I'll puff, and I'll huff, and I'll blow your house in."

So he huffed, and he puffed, and he puffed, and he huffed, and at last he blew the house down, and he ate up the little pig.

*T*he third little pig met a man with a load of bricks, and said:

"Please, sir, give me those bricks so I can build myself a house."

So the man gave him the bricks, and he built his house with them. Then the wolf came, just as he had come to the other little pigs, and said:

"Little pig, little pig, let me come in."

"No, no, not by the hair of my chinny chin chin."

"Then I'll huff, and I'll puff, and I'll blow your house in."

Well, he huffed, and he puffed, and he huffed and he puffed, and he puffed and huffed; but he could *not* blow the house down. When he found that he could not, with all his huffing and puffing, blow the house down, he said:

"Little pig, I know where there is a nice field of turnips."

"Where?" said the little pig.

"Oh, in Mr. Smith's garden, and if you will be ready tomorrow morning I will call for you, and we will go together, and get some for dinner."

"*V*ery well," said the little pig, "I will be ready. What time do you mean to go?"

"Oh, at six o'clock."

Well, the little pig got up at five, and got the turnips before the wolf came (which he did at about six o'clock). The wolf said:

"Little pig, are you ready?"

The little pig said: "Ready! I have already been and come back again, and I got a nice potful of turnips for dinner."

The wolf was very angry at this, but thought that he could trick the little pig somehow or other, so he said:

"Little pig, I know where there is a nice apple tree."

"Where?" said the pig.

"Down at Farmer Brown's orchard," replied the wolf, "and if you will not trick me again I will come for you at five o'clock tomorrow and we will get some apples."

*W*ell, the little pig got up the next morning at four o'clock, and went off for the apples, hoping to get back before the wolf came; but he had further to go, and had to climb the tree, so that just as he was coming down from it, he saw the wolf coming, which, as you may suppose, frightened him very much. When the wolf came up he said:

"Little pig, what! Are you here before me? Are they nice apples?"

"Yes, very," said the little pig. "I will throw down one for you."

And he threw it so far, that, while the wolf was gone to pick it up, the little pig jumped down and ran home. The next day the wolf came again, and said to the little pig:

"Little pig, there is a fair at Shanklin this afternoon. Would you like to go?"

"Oh yes," said the pig, "I will go. What time will you be ready?"

"At three," said the wolf. So the little pig went off before the time as usual, and got to the fair, and bought a butter churn, which he was going home with, when he saw the wolf coming. Then he did not know what to do.

*H*e was so frightened that he decided to hide in the butter churn. But when he got in it, it rolled down the hill with him inside, which frightened the wolf so much that he ran home without going to the fair. Then he went to the little pig's house, and told him how frightened he had been by a great round thing that came rolling down the hill past him. The little pig said:

"Ha, I frightened you, then. I had been to the fair and bought a butter churn, and when I saw you, I got into it, and rolled down the hill."

Then the wolf was very angry indeed, and declared he *would* eat up the little pig, and that he would come down the chimney after him. When the little pig saw what the wolf was about, he hung a big pot of water in the hearth and made up a blazing fire. Then, just as the wolf was coming down, the pig took off the cover, and in fell the wolf; so the little pig put the cover on again in an instant, boiled him up, and ate him for supper, and lived happily ever after.